My First Book about the Arctic Animal Alphabet

Amazing Animal Books
Children's Picture Books

By Molly Davidson

Mendon Cottage Books

I0439606

JD-Biz Publishing

Read More Amazing Animal Books

Purchase at Amazon.com

**Download Free Books!
http://MendonCottageBooks.com**

 is for an Arctic Fox

The arctic fox can survive in temperatures as cold as -58°F.

When there is a blizzard outside they will make a burrow in the snow, as a shelter to stay warm.

B

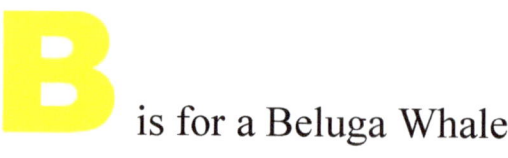

is for a Beluga Whale

Beluga whales live in the northern Arctic Ocean, but do migrate a little further south to the oceans surrounding Alaska, Canada, and Russia, when the ice freezes in the winter.

They can live up to 50 years in the wild.

C is for a Canadian Goose

Canadian geese live in the northern part of Canada and Europe during the summer, and then migrates to the south in the winter.

Canadian Geese mate for life, and lay 2- 9 eggs every year.

D is for a Dall Sheep

The Dall sheep lives in the North West region of Canada and Alaska.

They eat most plants, and in the winter they eat dried, frozen grass that sticks out of the snow.

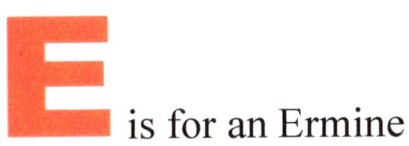 **E** is for an Ermine

An ermine is also called a short-tailed weasel.

Their fur is white in the winter and turns a brown color in the summer.

Ermine's white fur is worn by many royals.

F is for a Fur Seal

Fur seals can eat up to 10 pounds of fish in one day.

They have a thick undercoat on their bellies, which help keep them warm in the freezing temperatures.

 is for Greenland Sharks

NOAA © <u>Wikimedia Commons</u>

They live in the northern Atlantic Ocean around Greenland, Canada, and Iceland.

They like the water temperature to be from about 30 - 50°F.

They are the only shark that does not migrate to warmer water.

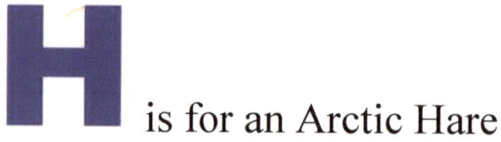 is for an Arctic Hare

The Arctic hare is also called the polar hare, because it is made for the cold. It has thick white fur and digs holes in the snow to keep warm and sleep.

They can run across the snow as fast as 40 miles per hour (mph).

I is for Insects

Eugene Eremeev © Wikimedia Commons

It is too cold for many insects to live in the arctic but some can survive just about anywhere.

Bees, wasps, plant lice, butterflies, moths, mosquitoes, and flies, are about the only insects you will see in the arctic, and some of those only come out in the summer.

**J** is for a Japanese Macaque

A Japanese macaque, or snow monkey, has a furless face and lives in the colder regions of Japan.

They can live in weather anywhere from 5°F up to 77°F, in the summer.

 is for a Killer Whale

Killer Whales live in every ocean throughout the year; they spend their summers in the southern Atlantic Ocean.

They live and hunt in large groups called pods.

L is for a Lemming

They live on the mountains and tundra of Norway.

Lemmings do not hibernate during the cold winter; they just burrow down to find grass, and eat some food they have stored.

 is for a Moose

Moose have a large habitat; they live in Alaska, the Rocky Mountains, Canada, Norway, Sweden, and many other northern European countries.

Moose can eat about 73 pounds of plants and shrubs per day in the summer; in the winter it is harder to find food, so they only eat about 34 pounds.

 is for a Norwhal

Glenn Williams © Wikimedia Commons

They live in the Arctic Ocean and do not migrate.

Scientists do not know the purpose of their tusk. It might be a way for the boys to attract the girls.

The boys have a much longer tusk than the girls some girls do not even have one.

 is for Odobenus Rosmarus

Odobenus Rosmarus is the scientific name for walruses that live on the ice of the Arctic Circle, in large herds of hundreds.

They use their tusks to help pull their large bodies out of the water, and to poke holes in the ice.

P is for a Puffin

Puffins can hold up to 12 small fish in their bills at one time, without eating them. This is so they can bring food back for their babies to eat.

Puffins talk to each other when they are in their colonies on land, but when they fly above the sea, they are silent.

 **Q** is for Quadruped Animals

A caribou is an example of a quadruped animal.

A quadruped animal has four feet; many arctic animals need four feet to stay secure on the ice.

Some popular quadruped animals are the polar bear, caribou, ox, fox, wolves, dogs, and many others.

R is for Reindeer

Reindeer, also called Caribou, live northern Europe, Russia, and North America.

Both the boy and girl reindeer grow antlers, which can be up to 3 feet tall.

They use their hooves to dig for food in the snow.

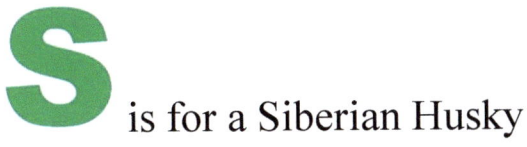

S is for a Siberian Husky

![Siberian Husky sitting in snow]

A Siberian husky has a thick coat of fur, which helps keep it warm even in below zero weather.

They are breed in North America, not Siberia, and used as work dogs, mainly for pulling sleds.

T is for a Tibetan Mastiff

Mimayin © Wikimedia Commons

The Tibetan Mastiff was bred to be a guard dog in the cold Himalayan Mountains for goats and sheep.

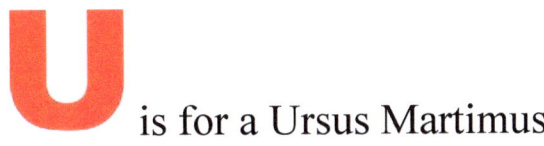 is for a Ursus Martimus

Ursus Martimus is the scientific name for a polar bear.

They live on the sea ice in the arctic. They are made to live here with their large furry feet and short, sharp claws that can easily grip the ice.

V is for a Very Snowy Owl

The Snowy Owl is also called the Arctic Owl; they live in the north of Asia, Europe, and Canada.

They will stay perched high and wait for prey to run across the snow before they fly down and snatch it to eat.

 is for a Woolly Mammoth

The Woolly Mammoth became extinct almost 45,000 years ago, it lived on the arctic tundra of northern Asia, Europe, and North America.

The African elephant is a cousin to the woolly mammoth.

X is for the Musk o

They live on the frozen arctic tundra and eat roots, moss, and arctic flowers.

They are about 5 feet tall, and weigh anywhere from 500 - 800 pounds.

Musk oxen live in herds that are lead by the girls.

Y

is for a Yellow-Eyed Penguin

Yellow - Eyed Penguins spend 3 out of 4 hours in the water, hunting for food.

Penguins live in one of the coldest climates; it can get down to -40°F, with wind speeds of 89 miles per hour.

Z is for Zooplankton

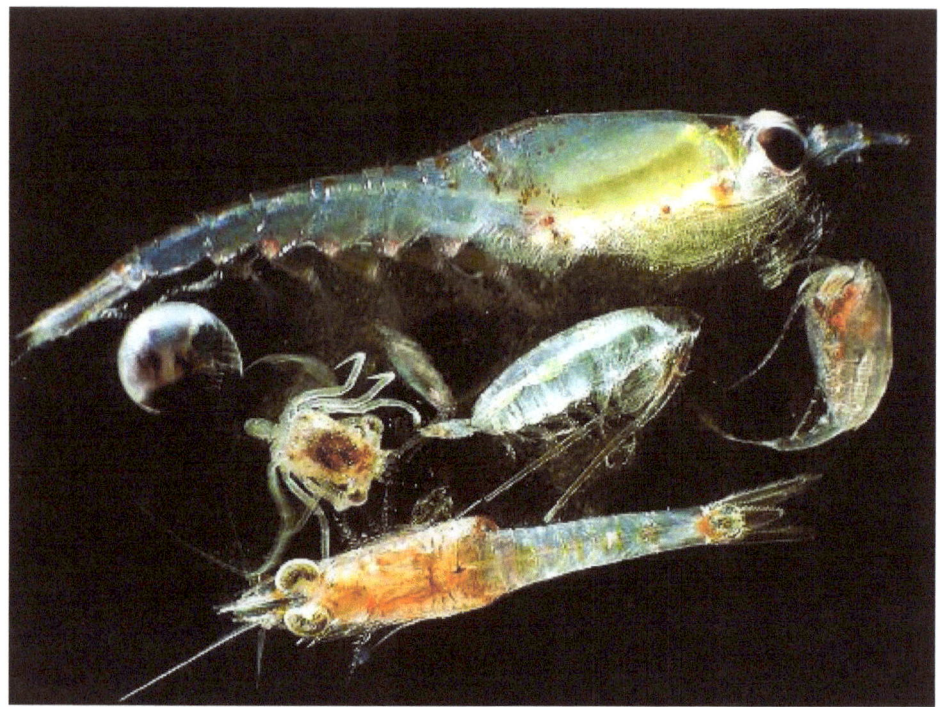

Matt Wilson/Jay Clark © Wikimedia Commons

Zooplankton are tiny animals that float through the ocean water, they are eaten by penguins and many other arctic fish.

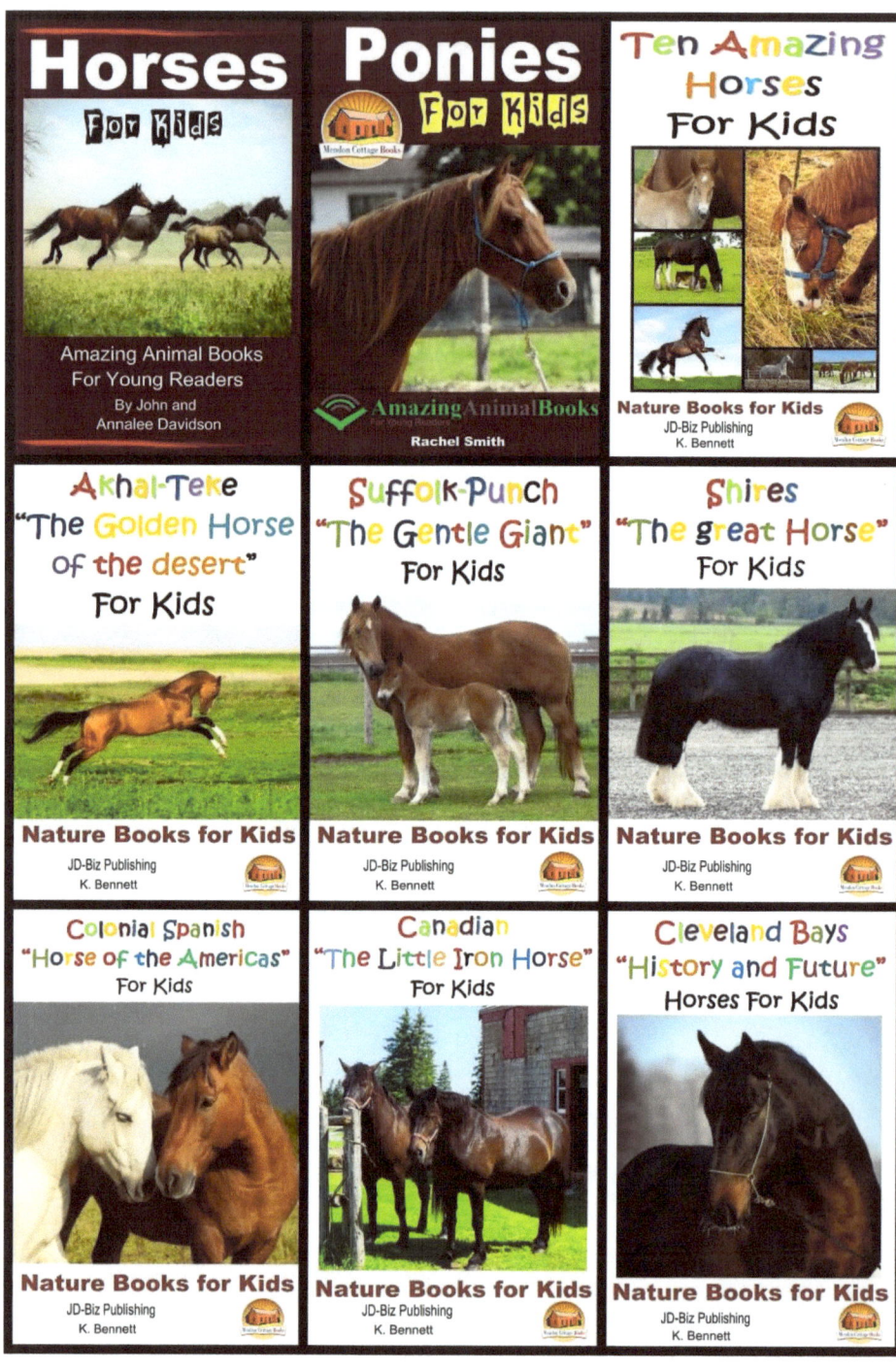

Our books are available at

1. Amazon.com

2. Barnes and Noble

3. Itunes

4. Kobo

5. Smashwords

6. Google Play Books

Download Free Books!
http://MendonCottageBooks.com

Publisher

JD-Biz Corp

P O Box 374

Mendon, Utah 84325

http://www.jd-biz.com/

Mendon Cottage Books

P O Box 374, Mendon Utah 84325

Mendon Cottage Books